GENESIS

JOHN POWELL WARD

seren

seren
is the book imprint of
Poetry Wales Press Ltd.
First Floor, 2 Wyndham Street
Bridgend, Mid Glamorgan
Wales, CF31 1EF

© John Powell Ward, 1996

Cataloguing In Publication Data for this book
is available from the British Library

ISBN: 185411-169-8

*The publisher acknowledges the financial assistance of the
Arts Council of Wales*

Cover Art:
Graham Arnold is one of the Brotherhood of Ruralists. Appearances
over four decades include the Tate Gallery, the Royal Academy and numerous
provincial galleries, and two one-man exhibitions at the Piccadilly Gallery in
London. His painting 'Genesis' was commissioned for this book.

Printed by: WBC Book Manufacturers, Bridgend.

Contents

Genesis

the evening the
the morning the

     trees
         fishes

and God said

and
         the fifth day

light on the waters

      man

the evening the
the morning the

Once

Once the world was vacant. No human
Owned it at all. Its primal
Order was nature too. Woods lay
Open to sky and the rare sunlight.
Only a few spots were inhabited.

Before we phased and spread our
Biggest settlements were hamlets.
Blue was the colour of all space.
Blue sea, blue sky, a high cobalt
Being itself the sole message.

Green briars were interspersed.
Green forests and ferns, and speckled
Green's torn vegetation; marsh;
Groves and doves and desert sands
Groping for the meaning of silence.

Who did own it then? What happened
When all chip was birds, the crackling
Weather thunder and the sheets of
Winter noiseless falls of snow,
Writing just footprints or blood?

Did God intend something? Was any
Deity around at all? No sound from
Deep time or deep space echoed
During those infinities. Was man's
Date of birth a bell, or silence too?

The earth must have felt more real
Than anyone who arraigns it. Yet to
Think such requires too the very
Tinge of being itself, the endless
Throb that here rents its human lodging

8

No matter what bush or doorway we
Nervously rest in forced to pass our
Night. Awesome it is to face that
Nothing ruled till our time, everything
New to us has accompanied all time.

Such brevity of life is chilling.
Spans of the hominoid are inches.
Soon having devoured this planet we
Shall go elsewhere, wondering, afraid,
Still unaware how to end, or begin.

Science Fiction

Dinosaurs first, aeons before our time.
Does it go always from big to small?
Deer, elephants and whales met their
Demise next, then lions and bears.

Smaller creatures disappeared
Supplying quotas of meat. Others
Simply ceased procreation. Wolves
Surrendered way back to the cold.

Foxes were drubbed out of life by
Farmers not without brief resistance.
Ferrets assisted with smaller prey
Flushing out their lairs. Then they

Went too followed by marmots and
Water rats. Salmon got hooked by
Water shortage or its pollution.
Weasels escaped into wire netting.

Toads were levelled by every kind of
Tyre that we invented. Hoopoes flew up
To the sky then glided down finding on
Tarmac no more slugs or worms. For

Ants also vanished now, some time
After the chafer's exit. Bees went mental
And killed their queens. Smaller termites
Ate each other, lacking flesh to feed on.

Briefly humans had casualties too, yet
Bearing in mind our expansion to many
Billions it meant little. All died out
Bar humans, we survived. All but humans gone.

Left so, research dwelt on physioneural
Life-support where nutrition is concept
Like mathematics. It was so calm at
Last. Other factors, even fear, diminished.

No problem, no 'upset balance of
Nature'. All was most gently ordered.
New-age man hence strode forward to
Notions of being hitherto unimagined.

The Night Surface

The fidgety, restless surface of
  The earth, where birds, disturbed,

Fly up and scatter, ants dart to and
  Fro and cars are shot like ammunition

Down sheets of tarmac, nothing rests,
  Dawn till dusk till midnight till dawn,

Nothing stills, nations snatch at sleep
  Non-stop, one by each one, on this turning

World like moths. Sleep, sleep — if once
  We feared death less and less

And felt the gulls and cars and cafe-lights
  As a cosmic eyelash, twitching, fluttering

In a pleasant dream in a relaxing mind's
  Infinite night, rear-lights of light.

Marathon

In rain, two hundred runners streaming
Past us yet so out of reach
It felt they or ourselves were dreaming.
Stirred, we drove ahead to watch
And parked. The hazels dripped. A man
Tore by at murderous cold speed,
Dead silent, pounding on the road.

Second and third ran powerfully.
Groups next with oddly awkward gait,
Their minds obsessed with healthful flight.
Then masses bunched and talkative
As amateurs, at play for love.
Then stragglers in threes and twos
And ones, mud splashing round their toes.

Later, through wheat, the thin white line
Far off, slow prisoners in a chain.
Earth's low flameless fire, their motion
Rhythmic as a crescent ocean.
In from the wet they took their showers,
Towelled, dressed, then out for home rejoined
Long marathons of crawling cars.

The Fifth Suit

My grandfather had these five three-piece suits.
I never saw him in any other thing.
The best was for annual dinner or wedding.
The second was 'best', Sunday and special nights.
His tailor cut them out exactly for him
From a striped grey, deep blue, and then some.

The third one the old man wore every day
In his working week. It was just as good
As the fourth, and when at the bus-stop he stood
In the queue he looked distinguished the way
Accountants used to. He wore a bowler hat.
On his office-door was a small brass plate.

You'll have guessed the fourth was his change
For the evenings, and the fifth was for gardening.
Foot on a spade, correctly attired, digging
With his jacket taken off now — he would arrange
It first on the back gate like a scarecrow.
But the one thing that we always never knew

Was the dreaded doom of the fifth suit every year.
For, once a year, he was fitted for a new one.
And all the five suits were relegated down
A slot — wedding to Sunday, Sunday to daily wear.
The fourth, at least still alive, went to the shed.
But the fifth, by God I shrank, for that suit was dead

And *never seen again*. We never saw it leave.
Cast into outer darkness, whirling and flailing
Its legs and sleeves, to the Milky Way in wailing
And gnashing of teeth, no fifth suit did ever survive.
Grandpa was chapel. I was haunted, I know.
Probably it went to Oxfam or that scarecrow.

So Far

apples are computers
beaches are creches
cars are loud-hailers
days are entitlement
earth is afternoons
fuel is decorum
grass is chrome yellow
hills are athletics
industry is sculpture
jeans are photography
kinship is unlikely
law is new physics
murder is abandon
neon is moonlight
offices are funtime
people are exceptions
quiet is recalled
rivers are fibreglass
sky is orchestral
tarmac is helium
understanding is microdot
victims are neighbours
water is consumption
x is all over
youth is authority
zeal is the extent

A Maybe Epitaph

Hung like a pin-point in the dark,
Huddles our reconstructed park.
Hopes revamping down from dreams.
How perfunctory it seems.

Earth contracts, each target place
Enters a final dose of space.
Endless gendering the test.
Every remaining grief expressed.

Scientists researching find
Something various in the mind
Sufficient for each probity.
Saviour dolphin, friendly tree.

Twist the roses from the light.
Time the crops to radiate.
Thank you speakers, never wrong.
Thank you singing, for your song.

Allocate what water's left,
Add survival's havering gift.
After noon the cosmic term.
Ash and swirl and nanotime.

Attempt

true story, 1993

This acquaintance had driven
To that land with supplies but
The resident murderers
Took away her driver

Whose head they sheared off
Whole at the dripping neck
Whereupon they kicked it
Whooping and playing football.

Once a holy man said we
Only ever suffer such
Onus as we are capable
Of bearing; this could be true.

Humour also played its part.
His amputated thing they
Held up like a grenade,
Hooraying the while.

Next month she went again,
Never one to back off from
New challenges or suchlike
Neurotic forebodings.

I must predict (she said)
I won't return this time.
Intuition mutters it's
Inconceivable, this time.

She was so nearly right.
Shelled from a low hill her
Small van was hurled
Sixty yards with her in it.

Mission over. And yet
Meanwhile each day since
More volunteers have gone in; as
Misguided, as foolish, as blind,

Carrying their boxes of
Comfort in these strange
Convoys of faint faith,
Clear on no destination bar

Action alone, as though to
Attempt such salvation
Aims at value itself.
At least get that through.

Two Weddings

The same noon but apart, siblings
Tor and Rill married their friends
Televising each other's weddings,
To record how that was very space
Their twosome made. Rill's event

Went ahead on a cliff-top. She
Wore robes that enfolded her but
Would soon unwind tonight. Tor's
Was far away in a tiny church
Wedged in an inland field of rye,

And the TV screen by his cool
Altar's step brought screaming gulls
And breaking waves to each of his
Assembled relatives. Meanwhile in
Accurate sync, the cliff-top

Screen was showing his church's pillars,
Scanning the vaulting, as Rill's
Swept guests glanced miles out to
Sea then back across Tor's wooden pews.
Stone muskily odoured, currents ebbed,

Field and sand-dune were both flung
Flat and long grasses smoothed them.
'For ever' sang the priest, 'For ever'
Foamed the brine, and one by one
Four mates drew close in a shared minute.

Lightness

Everything is lighter, weight along with
voltage. The electron outlasts the gantry.
The reeds stretch on the river's mud.
Music floats in the park like butterflies.

Millennium, but before that date the bulks
evaporated; buildings collapsed like
the old institutions lunching in them.
Dancing weeps and has gone soft again.

How vital, fields drowsing where jets
fly over more numerous but in silence;
silver streaks as with trout-streams below
ageing their reflections. Your cable comes true,

roots concealed, its arrival before its departure.
Cities extend their rings. If we emerge, on
stairs invented as we slide up them, our curse
stays with the daisies and bits of breeze-block

by unfinished hospitals and superstores. Children
read the menu of the dene and copse; the maps make
the places. The planet becomes rationale.
The creation's dew is the prism of its invention.

Computer Print-out

every evening in the twig twilight
in the sea's seams she washed and wished
in the sea's seams she washed and wished
every evening in the twig twilight

she flouted and floated her hair's air
the skein of her skin bare she bore
the skein of her skin bare she bore
she flouted and floated her hair's air

a manic man there stared and steered
her sharp shape to his brawny brain
her sharp shape to his brawny brain
a manic man there stared and steered

he strode and stroked her flashed flesh
her beast's breasts so soon seen
her beast's breasts so soon seen
he strode and stroked her flashed flesh

blessed bliss in the weaving waves
she became becalmed at his tough touch
she became becalmed at his tough touch
blessed bliss in the weaving waves

on the sand's land their play lay
sweetly sweating in a cove's love
sweetly sweating in a cove's love
on the sand's land their play lay

By the Sea

for E and J

Four tiny boys played
Football loudly on the blue
Foreshore. One would make some
　Mark we parents said.

Later their schools. Music,
Language, botany, sport.
Let me remember, let me prod
　My nights and days.

Girl-friends came and went,
Graduation and the great
Game of life. Its
　Milestones unnoticed.

One to medicine, one to law,
One to drama, one to craft.
Only sometimes they
　Met now, not forgotten.

Tragedy struck in their
Third decade when one was
Taken. He is their
　Miracle, he binds them all.

Taking Her Own

for J and in memory of C

Why? We gasp, crushed, stricken. Why?
Were those suburban wet farm-fields too empty?
Were some nailed headlines screaming?
Was age looming up, with a grey face?

Did illness lash, money fly away,
Danger lurk at the brilliant kiosks?
Dumb friends cut, home swamp? Or men not
Dare even mention such classed beauty?

'It wasn't that, really, none of that.
It was that my brain fell suddenly
Inwards, and from reality's splinters
I left hurrying for the warm night.'

Swim out, dearest, to your image,
Sleep softly in the ocean that you
So needed. So we whisper, gather here
Saying it, huddled beside your night.

In Memory

Carola: name
Arranged to
Remind heaven
Of your death and
Life. May words
Address eyes so

Calm departing
As to assuage
Remorse, as to cut
Out what pain
Led you inwardly
Away. Would your

Crushed world's
Aching heart
Rest now, dear
Oval face close its
Lids in good sleep
At such falling

Come quickly home.
Angelic: say it.
Ravishing: sing it
Openly and loud.
Lovely. Blonde. Begin
And end for us. Carola.

In the Country

to be alone now is
to be as a child
told parents were dead. it is
to see a seat with no one

sitting there, a field
scene with no person,
sunset with no witness.
seaside and the swimmers gone.

home is here, one's
house is warm, indeed
hearth and rug dispense
heat from the coal's

black solid. there are
books as before, one's
bedroom as before, to
be silent is now rare

proportion. currants and
plums give way to
passion-fruit, greenhouses are
plastic, weather-resistant

and grey. there's no
answer to such and none to
ask, the landscape's
arsenal of cars is

our voice and sole enouncement.
only the self propounds,
otherness is one's world
of orbit as of existence.

*

never despair friend,
no place derelict utterly,
nothing fully bereft.
now is the noon, the moment

for galactic blazes beginning,
fire burst and crackle,
fancies and fantasies,
flash, sparkle and flare

extended media-wise.
earth and ecstasy,
Eve her very self and
Eden too at last full-lettered.

aa bb cc dd ee ff gg
hh ii jj kk ll light
light light light light
light light light light

light li*ht light light
ligt light light light
lightXlight*light light
light light light light

light light light light
light light light light
light*light light light
light light light light

light light light light
light light*light light
lightS*light l**ight light
light light light light

*

26

iqzan blewo pcurj qvxde
fhkms tyaep dnxow htivm
rguyf bcjik lqszu*xrzjc
alvpm bnoxy dfgqt hkesw

light light light light
light light light light
light*light light light
light light light light

mmmmm mmmmm
mmmmm mmmmm
mmmmm mmmmm
mmmmm mmmmm

nnnnn nnnnn nnnnn nnnnn
ngngng ngngng ngngng ngngng
ooooo ooooo ooooo ooooo
ooooo ooooo ooooo ooooo

pqr s t u v w x y z
opq r s t u v w x y
nop q r s t u v w x
mno p q r s t u v w

pqr s t u v w x y z
opq r s t u v w x y
nop q r s t u v w x
mno p q r s t u v w

*

27

by the trees the twilight
begins rotation's work. night's
branches grey over, the hills'
bulge frightens them no more as

when everyone was here
with us but also each other.
where they are is no
wonder; now trees and soil come

in each year of our best
inception. younger and not sad
I know these magpies and grass
instinct with friendship and love.

Thanking Snow

for Anne Stevenson

Thanking snow
  For transforming
  Field and coasts,
  Forcing vision to where

Turning every single
  Molecule (says Davies) even
  Millimetrically would
  Make worlds

Twinkle and (bang!)
  Vanish. Such
  Veneer aged and
  Very certain:

Twigs and
  Earth in pots,
  Electric generator,
  Even this farm's sky

Takes on white, bears white,
  Such crushed white that even black
  Seems not itself but
  Snow's shadow.

That seems like
  Poetry. Poetry's
  Parabolic drift, its fall,
  Placing quotidian

Things under amazing
  Layers of
  Language till
  Left flat on

Top they too must change.
  All things remain
  As before yet subtly
  Altered. Subtly altered.

Thaw-time.
  Cars, B-roads and hedges
  Coated with mud and every
  Common sight again,

The air
  Gradually re-tinting
  Garages and back
  Gardens with their usual light.

Fragment

Life mends its colours,

Instruction,
Indigo.

Get a cathedral to the sea,
Green grass, maybe one
Garage. With some
Girls and boys too,

Have
Heaven

There

That Tree is Blue

That tree is moonlit blue, she said quickly.
But that is what I saw too he replied,
Nothing but that: the moon hanging low
With nothing but that cheetah-bird, bare
And with nothing but. That forked branch
Broken and with nothing but that a few black
Leaves broken and with nothing but that promise
She leaves broken and with nothing but that
Love she leaves. Broken and with nothing but
That *love she leaves, broken and with nothing*
But that *love she leaves, broken and with*
Nothing but that *love she leaves, broken and*
With nothing but that tree of love which is
Blue quickly, she said and oh I saw he replied.

October

C.C. d 14 October 1993
M.W. d 25 October 1993
P.V. d 29 October 1993

The details here are
True, as is the autumn
Time October: it was as I
Tell it: what I'm saying is true.

Again exploiting how our
Alphabet spreads and scatters,
Asking it to be the bits
And pieces, the twigs and leaves.

Both of us stunned but way
Beyond blaming anything; to
Be candid it's work to
Begin on 'green' or much else.

*

When the phone rang first
We were picking at cheese and grapes.
What is happening (defensively
We asked) to these decades?

Friends; close neighbours and
Farmers; his wife so inward
Flung herself that last morning
From the new bridge's girders

Into the airslip. It stands at
Immense height, the black water
Icy even for mid-October,
Ink near frozen. The city

33

Shone enchanted like her
Streaming hair and the bent
Smile of curiosity and calm
She always had, no more.

All of us falling into her
Abyss followed her, the very
Atmosphere there gyrated,
Attitudes spun, plans dipped.

*

When it rang the second time
We were here far west and secluded.
Woods with their trees all
Wonderful orange red and brown.

His voice high-pitched and thin.
His son in Auckland who driving
Had stopped to mend a tyre was
Hacked apart by a van on a country

Road at night. The boy's friends
Reached him in seconds. None
Recalled even a spasm. At least
Relief there was no pain, yet though

Vainly we wondered if soft
Views might settle, the cottage rest.
Various therapies; them maybe
Visit out here, regather here.

Groping from the car all three made
Grief's very image, in our rooms
Gave vent and clung then calmed.
Grass and low dunes held us,

34

Seashore the levels that we walked,
Sanding our feet as in the old days.
Sinking clouds failed twilight till
Sorrow fell and we drove them back.

Now flown home his ashes are interred
Next to a fellow-student dead
Newly of cancer. The stone church
Nestled by the cliff in trees: it did.

*

A third time that phone, exactly
As we entered the door: that
Actual minute: shock grips, more
Acute never happened, couldn't be.

Just for the record: debt already
Jumping him he uninsured (still no
Job) then 'was in collision with' a cream
Jaguar so later chose his way out.

Mindful a second (suicide too) as
Marx said is farce I add no
More here, the grievous
Moment enough for her scars.

*

Loved, dear, so close, so known.
Losses like this sear one, rinse, leave us
Limp and arbitrary survivors,
Lacking a plan, our projects' phases:

Rain-forest obliteration,
Research on the two-week embryo,
Radiation as cause of leukemia,
Ravaging tourist migrations —

It hangs right aside, such
Individual grief, from these ecological
Imperatives; they are the public tally
In figures of pain come home.

My letter-work too subsides (friends call it
Mania); fine as formal, suddenly it
Makes no sense from the heart,
Means nothing in silence. How do

You say what you feel, if all is internal?
You don't feel so much years older as
Years deeper. This realising, that
Yesterday they were alive but not today,

Crushes serenity. It is itself that
Car-crash we daily dread and live in
Constant terror of. It crumbles us.
Concisely, curtly, a torch is put out.

Everyone there who shoulders such
Extremity of grief — who also could
Eventually be struck down some such
Evening as, it chances, I write —

Helplessly watch, as theories evaporate,
Hoped proposals dangle, dear friends' days
Hollow out like their eyes for years ahead.
How we lack old wisdom a new way.

*

We can't unknow what has been found.
Worlds stud the night sky like dots or
Wheel almost invisibly slowly in
Wastes of tumescent space. There

Is no endless earth or ploughed
Infinite vegetation. No roots deep
In flat bottomless soil. The world
Is stressed like a bridge. Man's

Usual ancient sense of solid earth
Under our soles as our home's
Ultimate expression, is no more. How
Utter is one's love for these unpublic

Persons and single casualties.
Please planet please, save us; be
Placated by our late desperation.
Pardon our fateful expanse, our expense.

The Sea

How we all once watched it.
How it couldn't be built on.
How it swayed maybe under his feet.
How it couldn't be knelt on.

The pathless ways. No cafes!
The line of brine at night
Tickling the sand's bent belly.
Teasing us at our feet.

Day restored the wet gleam
Dripping the rollers down,
Deep from the black horizon.
Detail the sea has none.

Shapeless; measureless; no sanction;
Safe from the planner's whim.
Sinking, sinking, that was terror when
Swimming meant sink or swim.

Oil sends its rainbows out
Over the harbour's ebb now.
Oceans swell to absorb
Our lenient overflow.

Taking Leave

In taking leave again
I sign off from the sea,
Idyll but we must go
Inland where detail is.

Sea's width is a haven
Strange as that may sound.
Sound which is a sea word.
Strait which is a sound.

Direct and no way curved.
Driving rolls, the saloon
Doors banked out to the shoulder
During each motorway vigil

Not to crash or drop off.
Nobody knows. It was last
November that we swam,
Needing the icy water where

All our friends had been swept
Away. Not from us I mean,
As we had had love unending.
Atlantic is what I mean.

After Simone Weil

Gloucester

Suffering's no problem.
Simply bereaved or jobless.
Sanity floats alongside.

Affliction though is hell.
Accompanied by pain but also
Acutely numbed in its nature.

It is the sump of degradation.
It genders distaste and disgust.
It leaves you a half-crushed worm.

Christ himself was afflicted.
Crime and sin the excuse.
Compassion is impossible.

They don't want it even themselves.
They are condemned, condemned.
They stain us with their poisoned light.

Fathomless void, the afflicted are
Frozen to the soul so deep they
Feel never person again.

Brought there right from the start
By fact and matter's very
Being. Genes: some bastard: war.

Why this unspeakable blackness?
What Simone wrote on the subject
Weaves notions still barely credible.

Love being no dimension
Locates love no matter how far. Its
Lack no matter how near.

Therefore an infinite love
Treads infinity from God to God.
That's an awful lot of space;

No wonder atheists believe
Nothing else exists.
Nothing does, not materially.

On the other hand there's
Obedience. Of waves wrecking ships.
Of autumn leaves. Of sunlight.

This river's ripples, for instance.
The railway slices and glints.
Typists and roadmen eat snacks,

Absorb fast-food by the cathedral
And continue. Sun warms, it soaks.
'All the world down here is beautiful.'

Why the hell? Because choiceless.
Will needs will, said Nietzsche.
Won't work on coal. Can't kick the rock.

Yet the afflicted do see God?
You could say that, she tells us.
Yesterday's dream their dark star.

Time I went home. The car-parking
Ticket's expired. Love, pain,
Terror, light and evil. That's all.

The Annual Fair

at a college for the blind

What is a blind man's look?
  Is he thinking?

Maybe there's some kind of inward book.
  Maybe he's sinking

In a darkness several feet under
  With no window,

Friend an extrovert pink albino
  Hair white as snow,

Another girl's eyes sunk in the pits
  Of their sockets, wits

Gob-smacked. Eyeballs rolled up
  Into the skulls' top,

One eye stares, the other shut;
  Some smile, some not;

All beavering away at their projects.
  Gadgets:

Blind Scrabble set, blind chess,
  Edged trays for no mess,

Sensitized radio controls (not TV),
  White stick wired electronically;

They make outstanding piano-tuners
  We're told, masseurs, crooners

Even, or this one was, articulating
  Her thing

At this Blind College's Annual Fair,
  Guide dogs everywhere.

It is a perfect scene
  (for us I mean)

The mellow building with its gables.
  The bright green lawns and salad tables.

Nature

Spring

First week in dune, mourning due.
Phlox of sheep, there yous and lams
That haply gambled and barred.
The cheaping of birds, the sent of flours,

Spring whether in the hedge rose.
Routes that tern in the war
Mirth put fourth knew chutes,
Wight be loss am. The ere was wholly.

Summer

Son shone at hi noon, at lo tied
On the beech. Sum navel reck lay
In a creak from passed daze,
And serf broke on the sure.

Small buoys with spayeds played
Buy the see and built damns.
Turns swooped on muscles.
Inland, the waiving corn.

Autumn

Wry, maze and beens were in,
Buries hung in the lain and a well-healed
Girl road her hoarse upright.
Sun shone on September hays.

A prints was court and find,
Forbearing where he should knot bee.
The golden heir crumbled. No reign yet
In the blew hills of wails.

Winter

Moor friezing thyme. Bear trees
Weighted and there twigs broke at knight.
Eye sickles hung from Eve's and
Four too weaks no burred sang.

It was sew coaled, sew coaled.
The soil was pact like hard steal.
Owe that this to two sullied earth.
We red Frost to each other.

Tea Time

A blood-red teapot, apple-shaped, too plain
Beside a blue jug, urn-squared, cobalt-blue.
A plate with double-blue lines and a stain

Around a circular track, blue nuts, a few
Leaves hung in Navy blue (reflecting red
From the light's teapot) and the day a view

Of blue sea and a pink-red sunset shed
On a willow-patterned saucer and its cup,
A Chinese fence with strawberries abed,

By cherry trees and kingfishers flung up
At azure sky. Pagoda with my spoon
Across it like the humped bridge, girls, a pup,

A butterfly and tea. The afternoon
With cut bread spread with jam and raspberry,
Of flaking red and glass; we outstare alone

The peacock's world. A miniature tea-world.
Five billion times are you and me arranged.
Left motionless on china. If we could

All stay so, unpolluted, nothing changed.

Dusk

'Why do you even ask, why ever ever
Waste time on it anyway?...no
Wait a minute, no sweat, no way
Worldwide resource can near sustain
Whether planned or not, education nor
Work nor women, decision alone
Will make or bust this planet, that's
What has to sing, genetic law...'

For this was Christmas Day with enough
Food already devoured by us ten for a small
Famine relief. Cracker riddles discarded,
Funny hats and a debris of hazel shells,
Filthy pudding plates with brandy cream,
Five o'clock and long since dark.

Faces just visible in the candlelight.

Elegy for the Plank Man

*A man aged 66 was shot dead yesterday as he tried to stop a
raid on security guards by attacking the robbers with two planks
of wood.*

*Mr Donald Kell, a pensioner, lived with his wife in a council
flat 200 yards away in Finchley, North London.*

*As the robbers fled with £500 to a getaway car the father-of-two
lay dying on the pavement murmuring: 'What have they done to
me?'*

*He had been on his way to put up two 30in shelves for a
neighbour.*

*Commander John O'Connor, head of the Scotland Yard Flying
Squad, said 'The man was astonishingly brave. We will move
heaven and earth to find these people.'*

from The Times, Thursday, 27 July 1989.

Our earth spun like a dog shaking spume
Off its fur, rain-forests on fire for
Millions of pesos to arable and ash.
Maybe I've forgotten motorways maturing

For the first time. He was sixty-six.
Front-page news dying, a laughable leaf
Askew on the pavement, shot in his shorts and
Anonymous all through and then fame's fate.

Photo was a home-camera blow-up, he can't
Pose now. He smiles at disturbing distance,
Through frosted glass almost, a being beyond
Time in the blurred newsprint journalists enjoy.

Lugging his planks he reached Golders Green
Lloyds Bank. Two thugs 'in their 30s or 40s
Stockily built, unmasked and with beer bellies'
Suddenly rushed the security guards. Goodness,

If it exists, is very tiny, invisible even
It seems, a germ ill-advised and both those
Robbers sensed its flash when he just jumped
Right in with his plank. On his own, and said one

Mr Patel (who gave chase): 'He just came and came,
Madly, with his plank.' They punched and pushed
Him, kicked him to the ground but he returned,
Hoisting his plank like a triumphant tree

From which were shelves for a near neighbour.
For he helped people, his wife whispered.
A woman laid a blanket on the plank man
As he died murmuring, 'What have they done to me?'

Christ too with two timbers staggered and ended
Crucified, a robber each side. Curious coincidence,
That, chance no doubt but what wood I wonder
Twirled green for the plank man. For Finchley

Sweltered leafily that day. In hot hatless
Summer, lime avenue budding when a body
Reddened like a poppy, global greenhouses
Reversed a moment as businessmen, buses,

Pizza-Hut and Boots flared their foliage
Prior to exodus, the awakening weekend.
Couples on tour in England's last landscape
Cuddled in the grass, Gloucestershire grew

Lusher and Devon dreamed butterflies and bees.
Lakeland admired as everyone left London
Exhausted, roads clogged with tourism's traffic.
England slumped. 'What have you done to me, man?'

Letters

Came at the start as mere spaces.
Carvings on trees, scratches on stone.
Caves for small elves of meaning.

In time they found their own body.
Ink was letters' flesh, cool
Invention with one role and purpose.

Afterwards they went three-dimensional.
Actual objects; shop-fronts; wood
And card on the schoolroom floor.

Mobility followed; behind planes or
Musically gathered to appearance; young
Men and women choreographed in stadiums.

Eventually letters adjusted their
Existence to the computer. Sheer
Electronic impulse; when deleted, zero.

Will the genome be letter-shaped
Within us, genetically engineered?
Will an N soon mate with an M?

Song

Children are a home's heaven.
Children are a day's delight.
Created by our couplings in moonlight,
Caritas, so dear, to fulfil that
Craving for origin in everyman.

Then let's have two each and love
Them. If some want fewer still,
Terrific, the numbers go down.
There'll be an enshrinement in law
This decade, just wait, so we might

As well face it and get started.
And if (as happens) both parents die,
Adoption is the neat and easiest
Answer; some families of four
After all. For a lucky few.

If mothers don't want babes, why fine.
If this woman baulks at the prospect,
In camera for life, wracked with chores,
Inundated with cries, that fits also.
Indeed the fewer the merrier, so to say.

For the one planet will grow calmer.
Fields bloom radiant, and farms,
Fresh water fresh, oceans clear,
Factories a kind of artwork shop,
Fertility's electronic deployment.

Caritas, so dear, to fulfil that
Craving for origin in everyman,
Created by our couplings in moonlight.
Children are a home's heaven.
Children are a day's delight.

A Nature Poem

One child with a hole in its cheek.
One with a tape across an eye.
One with a plastic tube shoved up
One nostril, lying on its side
Oblivious. One crying with only
One leg. The colour of poppies.

Puffs of white cumulus in the sky.
Puffs of something else from the hill-ridges
Pounding the city with its tracer-streaks.
People running across the streets,
Possibly trying to view the scenery?
Poppies spread in a corn field.

Nature, great, the way the fir trees
Nurtured us and an old city
Nestled in the hills. You can see
Narcissus bent over his maps and more
Nimbus blobs overhead. You can hear
Nightingales where children scream.

Out Here

Driving out here through the louring twilight
I've come to dread. A horrid night

Of mind, some sickness when the nerves
Were punched sideways, your brain's car swerves

And never crashes, yet never rights.
On the PM programme the weatherman's reports

Before the hurricane are castigated again
('Don't worry, it will pass over Spain' —

Our lifelong hope). Then tomorrow's
Weather itself; my deepest fear; snow's

Coming so you will not, and fear
Of staying alone again, not knowing where

Home is, my friends or children are, or you,
Or whether that black nightmare of a year ago

Will return tonight, re-turn to white
Drifts that curve slowly, shine their own light,

Their moonlight into this remote house and keep
The motorways blocked, the track iced, the deep

Lanes of February dead, and crusted window sills.
Suffolk, Hereford, Ontario, West Wales,

The centrifugal thrust that hurls apart kin
Locked in this late twentieth century spin,

And now engendering something different.
A square page of snow. Time does not relent.

The Wye Below Bredwardine

The banks are steep. Drought. Water too low.
Too many trees by it too, it feels. Yet
They impress heavily, this hot calm day.
Trees hang and bulge over, and peer right down.
Thirsty alders lean over, the bane of water.

Huge plate-glass windows sliding along
Horizontally, slowly rotate as they go. No
Hurry in such drift. And when flies and seeds
Hit it, dartboards widen and meet the dead
Hauteur of the banks, their raw nettle clumps.

Lower down these panes bump submerged reefs,
Lazily give, yet resist quite breaking.
Little folds and pleats adjust the Wye's surface.
Leaning over you see its tiny corkscrewings,
Like pocks on estuary mud, but down water.

Suddenly, near one bank in a patch of weedy
Sunlight, a blue shoal of chub. And,
Several feet down by the bridge's piles, one
Salmon flickered deep like a neon light.
Swinging on a branch, a tyre half-submerged.

What ease has this tonnage of sedately moving
Water. Sleepily it stirs, then enfolded
With so slight a turn rolls over in bed and
Weighs sideways down again. A hundred metres
Wide. Leaves, bubbles, downy stuff, flies.

It is evening sunlight. Already. Lambs baa.
I love you sylvan Wye, or would do so,
If that were tenable, correct, and still allowed.
Instead, I say too many trees. Traherne himself
Imagined this heaven. Is there hope? Swans arrive.

Eden

let us plant a tree here, let us
imagine planting a tree/imagine
planting a tree here, where trees
already imagined lie/let us let the
trees be planted here where we lie/
just imagine how a tree planted here
might lie/we already imagined how
the sky just might be/let us plant sky.

over the moonlight. beyond the coaster.
level the daylight. open the dreamtime.
recount the instant. answer the doorway.
wander the forests. squander the moment.
wither the pressure. descend the spiral.
enter the canter. hinder the marvel.
pebble the shoreline. gather the berries.
ponder the sequel. follow the hunter.

the windmills settle on the grassy ridge,
and horses struggle to the drying stream.
the villagers assemble by the bridge,
and children dance and play their latest dream.
the animals absorb the sun's hot beam,
and fish in swimming feel the light of day.
the elders think of when the corn was grey
and mothers know things better than they seem.

Brief Moment

for Stevie Davies

Where do we go now? Where next,
When even hills skim past beneath us,
Weather is screened, all human
Work a lab retort and our one
World a comprehended place?

Traffic is depleted on the by-pass.
The dog barks. Rain on the shed's
Tin roof patters. I never expected
To hear such sounds again. Even
Thunder is a cracked certainty.

Oh we have a flight-path now. Bending
Over the sea's horizon we jet
On course to that last melancholy,
Our own starting-points. We are flung
Off yet stay absent where we are.

Abandoned and wet the forest lies.
As the eye swells the home shrinks
Accordingly. Vertigo spins and no
Assured foundation holds with
Arms outspread to catch us all,

Unable to fall. The ocean rocks
Under green and blue, its cargo's bulk.
Up through the night's dark track we stare,
Understanding hence that even there
Universes too can only stand and wait.

Over the Hill

Once we struggled up through wheat
Over the hill, heading for that
Orange the sun makes with its fresh
Outcropping warmth. Down below,

Very quiet under its drapes, the green
Valley awaited the day, which spoke
Volumes. I still can't plumb what
Vast ignorances this is coping

With, or how nations of the old
West might recover enough to give
Wisdom again as once they received it.
What speeds there are, what music.

Breathlessly we reached the top.
Bright dew had evaporated. A thin
Breeze rose from the Severn. Mountain
Bikes leant against a tree, with riders.

Numbers

Parched scrub, desert and a colossal hand
Pointing upwards, eighty feet in height.
Perhaps three million termites in one edifice.
Population as of cities, or the massed
People's Army of the second front. Yet no suburbs

To this monstrous habitat; yet too like us
They build the world instead of like
The mammals merging with their own, or
Tearing as a cheetah does some sixty miles
Through the jungle in a night, seeking prey.

Birds flock in thousands. They inscribe
Beautiful curves and harmonies in air; then
By a change of motion in the leader's mind
Bear down on shellfish breeding-grounds
Before the huge migration south, to sun.

Fish too, as when some great magnetic
Force suddenly shifts, whole shoals like iron
Filings sway and weave through the waves one
Fraction only, making a changed parabolic
Form in their gliding movement; just a touch.

Neither of these require a fixed abode.
Nor mammals in their hunting-hunted mode.
None but ourselves yet emulate such ants in
Nature, maybe unable to exploit them for
Nutrition so like them we must become.

Stars, stars; astral bodies in such numbers
Shine down on this church-like obelisk below.
Surely we are heading for twenty billion.
Structuring the globe, a garden first, to one
Single city, a holy city, a Jerusalem of hope.

Dust burns before the giant termite mound.
Distantly a herd of eland graze, a tiger
Dashing toward them while the sun bakes down.
Dots of something shimmer in the haze there.
Deserts stretch away, and away, and away.

Green

Goal! they roared.
He found the net
Under the stars
And the great floodlight.

The fans swayed
In their huge song.
Once more right
Had beaten wrong.

There is no moon.
There are no stars.
They are the slain.
The aeon's wars.

Because we run
Packing our shoes
Nose-to-tail
On the motorways

Down to the west
Still nose-to-tail
Seeking that green
Where all was well.

Anagrams are People

anagrams are people
a lemon rapes a grape

every leaf to come
a cemetery of love

whom Nelson Mandela won
one man who mends all now

o he entered dark Africa
oh dear friend take care

the ice-caps all melteth
the place calls the time

what is this our life?
this it for us awhile?

zones all widen, green fails
wells faze, lean origins end

Wind Machines Near Bridgend

Huge kisses on stalks. Kinder.
Skyline. Skyline. Skyline. Skyline.
Foxgloves. Blooms. smoolB. sevolgxoF.
Arms akimbo, semaphore. All-Stars.

Skyline. Skyline. Skyline. Skyline.
Angels, *aggeloi*, messengers from God.
New-born children. Axe to the root.
Larks rise, the spacemen have landed.

Tossing their heads in sprightly dance.
X is the spot. Bare range exchanges.
A thick hum emits from there all day
To those who go near or live so near.

They have come from a far country.
Etch not our awkward dialects.
Air is their food, their home is air.
Fluttering and dancing in the breeze.

Boxes. Ekko. Distaffs. Cool.
Crucify now and dance to the tree.
Hills asleep and under not asunder.
Am tallness to the tall blue blue.

Notes

The first two stanzas of 'Thanking Snow' use ideas from Paul Davies, author of books on the relations between religion, cosmology and science.

The poem 'After Simone Weil' refers to the essay 'The Love of God and Affliction', in Simone Weil, *Waiting On God*, Fontana 1950.

The technique used in 'Nature' was gratefully lifted from a poem by Josephine Abbott.

'Numbers' came from a photograph of a vast termite mound in Botswana.

Acknowledgements

Some of these poems have appeared in *Acumen, English, Interactions, The Interpreter's House, New Welsh Review, Orbis, Other Poetry, Poetry Nottingham, Poetry Review, Poetry Wales, The Rialto, Swansea Review* and in the anthology *Burning the Bracken: Fifteen Years of Seren Poetry* (Seren Books, 1996). One poem appeared in the author's exhibition POETRY OR TYPE at the Cardiff International and Kent Festivals of Literature, both 1993.